Praise for Great Bc

MW00626975

"If you've ever sat through a wandering, unproduc...
meeting and wondered, 'Why can't we do a better job?' read
Great Boards for Small Groups. With clean language, a wry sense
of humor, and a boatload of experience, Andy Robinson offers a
no-nonsense blueprint for success."

Paul Larmer, Executive Director
High Country News

"In addition to his deep knowledge, Robinson brings compassion for the struggles of newly-forming nonprofits. This book
combines inspiration and hope with practical, how-to advice."

Sister Guadalupe Guajardo, Sr. Associate Consultant
Technical Assistance for Community Services (TACS)

"An indispensable and accessible compendium of smart,
thoughtful and practical advice on how boards can best function
and be supported."

Tim Draimin, Executive Director
Tides Canada Foundation

"We keep a box of Andy's books in our office to share with
nonprofits. His ideas always resonate with both board and staff."

Virginia S. Martinez, Executive Vice President
El Paso Community Foundation

"Practical, concise, and a lively read. With this little book in
hand, you could certainly build and run a better board."

Paula Carrell, State Program Director
Sierra Club

"A great gift for board members, and bread on the waters for the
wise executive who gives it to them."

Ruth McCambridge, Editor in Chief
Nonprofit Quarterly

"I have witnessed first-hand the miracles that Andy helps
nonprofit organizations perform in Vermont. This book will give
you the tips you need to create your own miracles."

Jane A. Van Buren, Executive Director
Vermont Alliance of Nonprofit Organizations

The Gold Standard in Books for Nonprofit Boards

Read each in an hour • Quantity discounts up to 50 percent

Fund Raising Realities Every Board Member Must Face
David Lansdowne, 112 pp., $24.95, ISBN 1889102326

Nearly 100,000 board members and development officers have used this book to help them raise substantial money – in sluggish and robust economies. Have your board spend just *one* hour with this classic and they'll come to understand virtually everything they need to know about raising big gifts.

Asking   Jerold Panas, 112 pp., $24.95, ISBN 1889102172

It ranks right up there with public speaking. Nearly all of us fear it. And yet it's critical to our success. *Asking for money.* This landmark book convincingly shows that nearly everyone, regardless of their persuasive ability, can become an effective fundraiser if they follow Jerold Panas' step-by-step guidelines.

The Ultimate Board Member's Book
Kay Sprinkel Grace, 120 pp., $24.95, ISBN 1889102180

A book for *all* nonprofit boards: those wanting to operate with maximum effectiveness, those needing to clarify exactly what their job is, and, those wanting to ensure that all members are 'on the same page.' It's all here in jargon-free language: how boards work, what the job entails, the time commitment, the role of staff, effective recruiting, de-enlisting board members, and more.

The 11 Questions Every Donor Asks
Harvey McKinnon, 112 pp., $24.95, ISBN 1889102377

A watershed book, *The 11 Questions* prepares you for the tough questions you'll inevitably face from prospective donors. Harvey McKinnon identifies 11 such questions, ranging from "Why me?" to "Will my gift make a difference?" to "Will I have a say over how you use my gift?" And the suggested answers are illuminating.

How Are We Doing?   Gayle Gifford, 120 pp., $24.95, ISBN 1889102237

Until now, almost all books dealing with board evaluation have had an air of unreality about them. The perplexing graphs, the matrix boxes, the overlong questionnaires. Enter Gayle Gifford, who has pioneered an elegantly simple way for your board to evaluate and improve its overall performance. It all comes down to answering a host of simple, straightforward questions.

Big Gifts for Small Groups
Andy Robinson, 112 pp., $24.95, ISBN 1889102210

If yours is among the thousands of organizations for whom six- and seven-figure gifts are unattainable, then in this book you'll learn everything you need to know to secure big gifts: how to get ready for the campaign; whom to approach; how to ask; what to do once you have the commitment; even how to convey your thanks in a memorable way.

Emerson & Church, Publishers
www.emersonandchurch.com

Great Boards for Small Groups

A 1-Hour Guide to Governing a Growing Nonprofit

Printed in the United States of America

ISBN 1-889102-04-0

10 9 8 7 6 5 4

This text is printed on acid-free paper.

*Copies of this book are available from the
publisher at discount when purchased in
quantity for boards of directors or staff.*

Emerson & Church, Publishers
28A Park Street • Medfield, MA 02052

Library of Congress Cataloging-in-Publication Data

Robinson, Andy.
  Great boards for small groups : a 1-hour guide to
governing a growing nonprofit / Andy Robinson.
      p. cm.
  ISBN 1-889102-04-0 (pbk. : alk. paper)
  1. Nonprofit organizations—Management. 2. Boards
of directors. 3. Voluntarism—Management.
4. Charities—Management. 5. Fund raising.
I. Title: Governing a growing nonprofit. II. Title.
  HG4027.65.R628 2006
  658.4'22—dc22

                                  2005034874

Great Boards

for Small Groups

*A 1-Hour Guide
To Governing
A Growing Nonprofit*

Andy Robinson

Emerson & Church PUBLISHERS

ACKNOWLEDGMENTS

After 25 years of working with nonprofits, and more than a decade of consulting and training, I can say with confidence that there are very few original ideas about how to build a successful organization. The occasional flash of insight is a fine thing, but the best wisdom always begins with clear observation and is grounded in common sense.

Those of us who assist nonprofits tend to borrow from each other and adapt based on what we learn. If we're lucky, we might find a new way to address an ongoing problem, which we return to the common pool of knowledge for more experimentation and conversation.

To my many, many colleagues: thanks for sharing. I am humbled by your generosity, and I offer this book in the same spirit.

For Jan, with love

Big Gifts for Small Groups

Andy Robinson • $24.95 • 112 pp., $24.95
ISBN 1889102210

If yours is among the tens of thousands of organizations for whom six- and seven-figure gifts are unattainable, then *Big Gifts for Small Groups* is just the ticket for you and your board.

Robinson is the straightest of shooters and there isn't one piece of advice in this book that's glib or inauthentic.

As a result of Robinson's 'no bull' style, board members will instantly take to the book, confident the author isn't slinging easy bromides.

They'll learn everything they need to know from this one-hour read: how to get ready for the campaign, whom to approach; where to find them; where to conduct the meeting; what to bring with you; how to ask; how to make it easy for the donor to give; what to do once you have the commitment; even how to convey your thanks in a memorable way.

Robinson has a penchant for using precisely the right example or anecdote to illustrate his point. By the end of the book, your board members just may turn to one another and say, "Hey, we can do this" – and actually mean it.

Emerson & Church, Publishers
www.emersonandchurch.com

CONTENTS

1

Your Best Board

If you're joining your first nonprofit board, welcome to a new world.

Across the country and around the globe, some of our most important and enduring work – break-throughs in science and medicine and education, movements for human rights and social justice, artistic achievements great and small – has been conceived, birthed, and nurtured by nonprofits.

Compassionate organizations, often understaffed and struggling to survive, hold our communities together.

Working through their groups, board members dream ambitious dreams, foster great accomplishments, cope with deep disappointments, and practice a lot of "muddle-through management."

If you're already a seasoned trustee, you know that boards can be great repositories of wisdom, expertise, and fellowship. They can help you develop new leadership skills while providing the satisfaction of working together toward a shared goal. They can also be dysfunctional in multiple ways. Indeed, many boards are terrific in some respects and miserable in others.

Perhaps you're reading this book because you want help with board problems – and I am happy to report that you've got the right book. My goal is to help you to address the challenges you face as an individual leader, and also as a group of volunteers working together toward a common purpose.

In thinking about these challenges, however, it's wise to begin with a vision of success. What would your "best board" be like? What can an effective, cooperative, and hard-working team of trustees bring to your organization?

Here's my short list:

1) *Compliance with the law.* Assuming that your group is incorporated, you're required to have a board to oversee your programs and finances. The laws relating to nonprofits are designed to ensure that charitable organizations benefit the community at large, not just one individual or a handful of people.

This is the essential distinction between for-profit businesses and nonprofit corporations. At the most basic level, a board of directors (sometimes called a board of *trustees*) creates community ownership of the organization and provides a counterweight to individual self-interest. The community owns the organization, with the board as its representative.

2) *Free labor.* In most organizations, board members receive no compensation – they function as a pool of committed volunteers. Few grassroots groups could survive without the time and energy donated by their board members.

3) *Representation of the constituency served.* The most ethical groups, and often the most successful ones, are led by those who directly benefit from the organization's programs. To do their best work, anti-poverty agencies need poor people among the leadership, arts organizations should include artists, and groups that serve the disabled would do well to include those with disabilities (or perhaps their family members) on the board.

4) *Perspective.* Because trustees are less involved in day to day operations, they can view program activities from a bit of a distance to ensure that the group is meeting its mission.

5) *Long-range planning.* The board helps staff to weigh options and choose the future.

6) *Fundraising planning and implementation.* In healthy organizations, board members assist with the development of a fundraising plan and participate in

13

raising money by honoring and implementing the plan.

7) *Mutual support and encouragement.* The best boards are "learning communities" where people are encouraged to try new skills, take risks, and share responsibility for both victories and problems.

8) *Succession planning.* Good boards promote new leadership by actively recruiting and grooming new trustees and, if necessary, providing a gentle push toward the exit for those who have served too long.

•••

If this strikes you as an ambitious list, you're correct. The success of your board will be determined, in part, by your collective ambition. It's easier to create a great board if you strive to be great. If you settle for mediocrity, that's what you'll get.

2

The Evolving Board

How governance changes
as organizations change

Most organizations begin as "kitchen table" groups: a bunch of neighbors sitting around somebody's kitchen, trying to solve a common problem or meet a community need. These folks share a passion for the cause and a willingness to roll up their sleeves and do the work. They're seldom skilled in nonprofit governance and frankly, they don't even think about that stuff. They just want to fix what needs to be fixed.

Sometimes these informal groups continue for years or decades without growing or changing significantly, and their familiar leadership structure continues to serve them well.

In other cases, they want to expand their impact, so they decide to hire staff and open an office. My colleagues at the Institute for Conservation Leadership call this stage "the leap," and it's filled with peril.

Organizations hiring their first staff must address issues such as:

- Now that we have an employee, how does our role as a board change?
- How do we serve as supervisors without micromanaging?
- How will we ensure that our staff has adequate resources to do the job well?
- How do we evaluate our programs, our staff, and each other?

At this stage, other problems may surface as well. Board members who got involved because they care about the issue are suddenly responsible for personnel policies, staff supervision, a more detailed level of planning, and greater responsibility for fundraising. The visionary leader(s) who founded the organization may be unwilling to share power with the staff, which can lead to conflict, confusion about roles, and employee turnover. Or maybe the board breathes a collective sigh of relief, backs away, and abandons its responsibilities, assuming the sole employee will do everything.

As you can see, the skills needed to start a group are not the same ones needed to take it to the next level of effectiveness.

As nonprofits continue to grow, expand programs, and hire more staff, the board's role continues to change. Because organizations become more complex, board governance also becomes more complicated. In the ideal model, sometimes called shared governance, the board and staff share power and responsibility, are clear about their respective roles, and have systems in place to create orderly transitions as people leave and new ones come in.

At this phase, the board has explicit written agreements that define what is expected of each trustee, and what he or she can expect in return. (You can read more about board agreements in Chapters 5 and 6.) These groups have a culture of accountability and mutual respect; they also have fun together and celebrate their shared accomplishments.

As you can see from this chapter, board requirements and behavior must evolve as organizations develop and change. No single "right way" will be relevant to all nonprofits, or even to a specific organization at different stages in its life.

Rather than a set of rules, this book offers a menu of ideas and strategies to try with your own group. Feel free to experiment. Choose the ones that best meet your needs and circumstances.

3

Board and Staff

The separation of powers

Imagine your organization is lost in the jungle. You're tying to find your way to the coast where rescue awaits. Under those circumstances, who does what? Your trustees should be up in the treetops, pointing in the right direction. "Over there! Head east!" Meanwhile, the staff members are down on the ground with machetes, clearing a path by chopping through the undergrowth.

Or perhaps you fly into New York City and hire a taxi. You say to the cabbie, "Take me to the Metropolitan Museum," but you wouldn't insult the driver by instructing him at every turn. In this case, the board is the passenger – identifying the destination – and the staff is the driver – figuring out the best route.

For many board members, the hardest part of the job is determining where their responsibilities end and staff work begins. Unsure of their role, trustees may attempt to control every operational detail (we call this *micro-management*) or disengage and leave employees to make nearly all decisions (known as *rubber-stamping*). The ideal balance is somewhere in between.

To help you to think more specifically about who does what, review the following table:

Board Responsibilities	**Staff Responsibilities**
1) Makes final decisions on policies relating to mission, programs, finances, personnel, and public relations.	1) Carries out work authorized by the board or other policy-making bodies (for example, the executive committee).
2) Provides leadership and expertise with technical needs as identified by CEO and staff: for example, legal, accounting, marketing, and fundraising.	2) Provides the professional skills needed to manage daily operations.
3) Expected to know the mission, history, policies, and programs of the organization.	3) Responsible for understanding and mastering his or her own job.
4) Expected to know the duties the board delegates to staff.	4) Makes day-to-day decisions necessary for the functioning of the organization.
5) Available for staff consultation on matters of mutual concern.	5) Consults with board as necessary on program, finance, strategic planning, fundraising planning, and other issues.
6) Acts as both an informal and, when requested, formal ambassador and spokesperson for the organization.	6) Performs outreach duties as outlined in his or her job description.
7) Hires and evaluates the executive director.	7) The executive director is responsible for hiring and evaluating other staff.

Continued on next page

Board Responsibilities	Staff Responsibilities
8) Ensures financial support by participating in fundraising planning and activities, including making a personal gift.	8) Supports the board in its fundraising duties. Working through the lead staff, carries out fundraising tasks as assigned.
9) With the help of the staff, evaluates and updates the work of the organization to ensure that it is meeting its mission.	9) Helps the board make good decisions based on complete, accurate, and timely information.

Of course, each organization interprets these guidelines a little differently (or chooses to ignore them altogether). It's up to you and your fellow trustees to sort out the details. If you take the time to work out a clear, explicit, and commonly shared framework for who does what, you'll have a lot less confusion and conflict.

4

"Why Did They Ask Me?"

That's a great question. Why *were* you asked to join the board?

Maybe you've already shown commitment to the cause by volunteering your time or contributing money. Perhaps you have a special skill – public relations, event planning, facilitating meetings – the organization needs, and the other leaders hope to tap your expertise. Maybe you've directly benefited from the group's work, so you can add a useful perspective on the value of its programs. Or maybe you're rich and the board hopes you'll bail the organization out of its financial crisis.

More than likely, one of the board members knows you personally and simply thought you'd be a good fit.

Whatever the reason, you'd better ask. And if you don't get a satisfactory answer – in other words, if their expectations don't match yours – feel free to say no. In the long run, everyone will be happier.

5

"Can I See
A Job Description?"

If you're like me, you've probably taken a new job without having a complete picture of your responsibilities – in other words, without seeing a job description first.

Undoubtedly you encountered workplace surprises, not all of them pleasant. You may have ended up wishing you'd had a better understanding of the work before you accepted the post.

Board service is a job, too. Like any job, it has specific requirements and responsibilities. You're a volunteer, so don't expect to be paid, but you have the right to expect other forms of compensation: a sense of fulfillment, the opportunity to learn new skills, and the privilege of being part of an effective team. You might even be invited to cool parties.

Nearly all successful boards have some sort of "job description" or "board agreement" or "board contract."

The best of these documents are reciprocal: they spell out what you're expected to do and what you can expect in return. (A sample is included in the Appendix.)

A clearly-drawn board agreement is helpful in several ways.

• It sets common expectations and levels the playing field among board members.

• It provides a basis for evaluating individual trustees and the board as a whole.

• It can serve as a pry bar to gently remove ineffective board members who aren't meeting their collectively agreed-upon responsibilities.

• It's a great tool for recruiting new board members.

Now, you may be thinking: if we specify what we want, and provide all that detail, we'll scare away potential board members who can't fulfill our expectations. Well, if people can't meet their obligations, would you rather find out *before* or *after* they've been voted onto the board?

In my experience, the opposite happens. A clear, concise board agreement is attractive. Prospective trustees review the document and say to themselves, "Wow, this group is *organized*. It's impressive how they've thought through this stuff. I bet this is a great board." And you know what? It probably is.

6

Reciprocal Board Agreements

What you give, what you receive in return

If you've ever tried to complete a task without the right tool – we could be talking about cooking or carpentry or operating your computer – you've undoubtedly felt frustrated. In the same way, our service as board members can be frustrating if we lack the tools we need to do the job effectively.

An example: by joining the board, you've accepted fiduciary responsibility for your organization, which means you and your fellow trustees must ensure its financial health and integrity.

The problem is, you don't really understand the financial statements distributed at each board meeting. (This may be embarrassing to admit, but believe me, you're not alone.) The missing "tool," in this case, is the ability to interpret the numbers and evaluate their implications.

As a board member, you can't do your job without adequate training and support. Any meaningful job description must be *reciprocal*: it defines what is expected of you, but also what you can expect in return. Here's a sample excerpt:

Board member responsibilities	What board members can expect in return
I accept fiduciary responsibility for the organization and will oversee its financial health and integrity.	I expect timely, accurate, and complete financial statements to be distributed at least quarterly, one week in advance of the relevant board meeting. I also expect to be trained to read and interpret these financial statements.

As you can see, this approach provides fewer opportunities for misunderstanding, because the specifics are covered in enough detail to make everything explicit. Here's another example that covers meeting attendance:

Board member responsibilities	What board members can expect in return
I understand that the board meets six times per year, plus one annual full-day retreat. I will do my best to attend each meeting, with the understanding that three consecutive unexcused absences will be considered resignation from the board.	I expect that board meetings will be well run and productive, with a focus on decision-making rather than just reporting. I understand that agendas will be distributed at least one week in advance. If I wish to add items to the agenda, I will contact the chair at least two weeks in advance.

Perhaps you're thinking, "Boy, this seems so formal. Our group is much more relaxed. If we set specific rules – and hold people to them – it's going to feel a lot different around here."

You're right: it *will* feel a lot different: less confusion, fewer unspoken assumptions, more accountability. It will change the culture of your group. However, informality and clear expectations aren't mutually exclusive. If you work it right – for example, creating an explicit job description, but also reserving time in your meetings for food, stories, and celebrating the mission – you can have both.

A sample board job description can be found in the Appendix. Use it as a template, not a mandate. Play with the model and adapt it to suit your needs. Perhaps you can make the language less formal, but still define everyone's shared responsibilities.

Use this document as an opportunity to discuss what you expect of each other. The more you debate and revise it, the greater your sense of ownership. If you build it, you own it.

7

The Gift of Time

How much is enough?

While board members must give financially to the organization (see Chapter 18), perhaps your most important contribution is the gift of time. Given our families, jobs, commutes, and social obligations, personal time is a shrinking resource, which makes it ever more precious.

It surprises and saddens me that so few boards have explicit guidelines about the time commitment involved. Many trustees assume that if they attend all board meetings, they will have fulfilled their obligations. There's no discussion about preparing for meetings, committee work, fundraising, participating in organizational events, and other tasks that spring up over the course of the calendar.

Since nonprofit needs are wildly different, I'm wary about estimating the number of hours required. At one end of the spectrum, I know committed board members who invest 40 hours per month or more. At the other end are trustees who carefully choose their commitments – and these individuals can be very effective in their self-limited role. Overall, the typical board member probably contributes five to ten hours per month.

What's the right number for your group? Put this item on the agenda and have a frank discussion. You could also check with peer nonprofits. Do they have explicit time requirements or benchmarks for their trustees?

Even if you ultimately "decide not to decide," the conversation will help to clarify what people want and expect from each other, and from their service on the board.

8

Designing Your Best Board

Try this exercise:

Gather your fellow board members around an easel and flip chart, or large pieces of paper taped to the wall. Ask the following question:

"If we could design the perfect board for our group, what skills and qualities would we look for in prospective board members?"

Skills would include specific expertise to help the board run effectively: program knowledge, marketing, fundraising, consensus-building, and appropriate professional wisdom (for example, accounting, community organizing, investment, or legal knowledge).

Qualities would cover more intangible – but no less important – factors such as personal experience as an agency client, sense of humor, team player, good listener, willingness to attend meetings, risk-taker, experience on other boards, and diversity in terms of race, social class, gender, age, geography, and sexual orientation. Perhaps the most important criterion is passion for, and commitment to, the nonprofit's mission.

Brainstorm this list with the full board. Think as broadly as possible. With a bit of effort, most groups can generate 25 or 30 items they would love to incorporate into their "best board."

Having created this list, it's natural to ask, "How does our current board compare to this idealized one? What are we doing well? Where do we need help?" At a more sophisticated level, you might ask, "How do we recruit a different mix of board members to fill the gaps we've identified?"

If you're ready to continue to the next stage of this exercise, review the list together and give yourselves a collective grade for each item. At the end of this book I've included a blank matrix, like the one below, to assist you.

You can also use this exercise as a tool for self-evaluation. Ask each board member to rate himself or herself against the criteria on the list, using the same scoring system. This exercise helps leaders to think more creatively and comprehensively about what they bring (or don't bring) to the board. As a result, it provides an opportunity to help improve or remove less-than-effective trustees.

As a third option, you could ask the officers or the board renewal committee (if you have one; see Chapter

11) to fill in the sample matrix. Using this approach, the committee copies the brainstormed list down the left side of the form, adds the initials of board members across the top, and scores each member individually against the criteria created by the full board. Here's a partial sample; in practice, your list would be somewhat longer.

Skills & Qualities Desired **Board Member Initials**

	LT	AL	RS	MI	AP	NT	GS	PR	SS	HF
Has much time to volunteer	-	?	+	+	+	✓	-	+	?	✓
Will come to meetings	✓	?	✓	+	✓	+	-	✓	-	+
Program expertise	+	-	+	✓	-	✓	+	✓	?	+
Is a team player	-	-	+	+	+	✓	✓	+	?	-
Experience on other boards	+	+	✓	-	+	-	-	✓	+	?
Fundraising skills	-	+	-	-	?	-	+	✓	+	-
Meeting facilitation skills	+	?	✓	✓	?	✓	?	✓	?	-
Accounting/financial skills	+	+	-	-	✓	✓	✓	-	✓	✓

KEY: (+) Outstanding (✓) Adequate (-) Poor (?) Don't know

Once this work is completed, the committee would give the full board an overview of its findings, leaving individual scores anonymous. Committee members could also meet with individual trustees to show appreciation for the things they do well and brainstorm ideas for improving their weaknesses and increasing their participation.

This third approach makes some folks nervous, because it allows one committee to judge the work of everyone. If this doesn't feel right for your group, pick one of the other options.

9

Where Do Board Members Come From?

To be effective, board recruitment must begin with a "gap analysis" as outlined in the previous chapter. By identifying the weaknesses and blind spots on your board, you can actively seek out people to fill those gaps.

Are your meetings unproductive? Look for prospective trustees with meeting management skills. Not enough board fundraising? Recruit board members who aren't afraid to ask for money. Does everyone on your board come from the same neighborhood and social class, and therefore everyone has the same assumptions? Maybe it's time to look beyond your circle of friends. Here are several places to start your search.

Your clients, customers, and audience members. People who benefit from your work – or perhaps their family members, depending on your constituency – have a uniquely useful perspective on your organization. In fact, some organizations require that clients serve on the board.

Your members and/or donors. By making a financial contribution, these folks have already demonstrated their dedication to your mission.

Your volunteers. By donating their time, volunteers have also shown significant commitment.

Your committees. Smart nonprofits use their committees in the way professional baseball teams use their farm systems, by including non-board volunteers in committee work. If these volunteers prove themselves at the committee level, you can promote them to the "major leagues" and ask them to join the board.

Other nonprofit boards. Many people serve on multiple boards, so study annual reports and newsletters from other organizations. If this feels like raiding talent, feel free to cultivate these individuals now and recruit them later when their current board commitments are completed.

Professional associations and networks. People active in professional associations – fundraisers, human resource managers, technology specialists – can add appropriate expertise.

Public officials. With some organizations, it makes sense to include elected officials and government employees. In others – for example, nonprofits that work to challenge and change government behavior – it may be inappropriate.

Your friends. It's fine to approach your friends, as long as they feel passionate about the mission, can help to fill some of the gaps you've identified on your board, and will agree to honor the job description. However, it might be wise to resist the urge to *begin* by recruiting the people you know best.

Notice the people who are *not* included in the above list.

Rich people. Everyone's favorite fantasy: if we recruit the rich, they'll bring lots of money with them. This serves as a convenient excuse for other trustees to avoid fundraising, which is surely part of the job. (See Chapters 18 through 22.)

"The well-connected." While it's useful to have board members who can open doors on your behalf, before they can effectively do so – and often before they are *willing* to do so – these individuals must feel committed to your group.

To be fair, well-off and well-connected people can appear in any of the categories listed above: other boards, services organizations, public officials, even your own membership and volunteer base. However, if you single them out because of their wealth or connections, rather than their passion for the mission, you're courting disappointment.

Anyone we can get. Desperation won't work in your personal life, and it surely does not work when recruiting leadership. If you don't expect much, you won't get much.

10

"How Do We Ask Them to Join Our Board?"

How were *you* recruited for the board? You said yes, so something about the request must have worked. Was it a personal appeal from someone you respected? Did the recruiter suggest that you had unique skills or qualities that would enrich the board? Were you excited to accept, or did you feel a tinge of apprehension? (Perhaps both.) Were you encouraged to ask questions and speak frankly about your concerns?

The most effective recruiting strategies are specific and straightforward. To recruit your new leader, choose from among the following tools and techniques.

Conduct an interview. This obvious first step is neglected far too often. Set up an appointment with the candidate to discuss your organization, your board, and why you're asking him or her to join. If you've chosen someone who is already active in the group – as a volunteer, committee member, or donor – ask about why he or she has chosen to become involved.

Share your board job description. Talk the prospective trustee through this document (see Chapters 5 and 6, plus the sample in the Appendix). Emphasize that board members give a lot to the organization, but receive a lot in return.

Ask the candidate to fill out a board application form that explores the prospect's commitment to your mission, skills he or she could contribute to the board, and so on. An example can be found on page 108. It might be helpful to review the form together before the candidate fills it out.

If the idea of an "application" seems too formal for your organization, don't use one. It certainly isn't required. However, the process of answering application questions offers another chance to clarify everyone's expectations. The form may scare off a few prospects, but in the long run that might be a good thing.

Invite the candidate to observe a board meeting then sit down together afterward to debrief and answer any questions. If you're concerned about confidentiality, schedule sensitive topics when no guests are present.

Ask other trustees to provide their own perspectives. Encourage candidates to talk with several board members about their experiences on the board.

•••

The best approach always includes a simple request for help: "We need you. You'd make a terrific addition to our board because...."

And you know what? People like to be needed.

11

Board Renewal

Good work that never ends

On many grassroots boards, recruitment is left to the nominations committee, typically a small group that takes on the task of identifying prospective board members.

Here's a typical process: the committee asks the full board to suggest names, receives no response, gets frustrated, waits for the next meeting, asks again, gets one or two names, feels disrespected, comes up with a few additional candidates on their own, makes a few phone calls, and brings the proposed slate to the board.

During the brief discussion that follows, most participants have no concrete way of evaluating the candidates and are forced to rely on informal references provided by their peers: "Trust me, she'll be a great addition. She's rich." Or maybe, "Jim would be useful, since he knows everybody in town." Once the nomination process is complete, the committee goes into hibernation until the next year.

Having filled out your board matrix as described in Chapter 8, you should understand that nominations must be *intentional* – you're looking for individuals who can meet specific needs. If you go out and corral people at random, you subvert the purpose of the exercise.

The real care and feeding begins once people join the board. To address this need, many groups are moving from a nominations committee to a *board governance* or *board development* or *board renewal* committee. Rather than perform a single task once per year, this committee has a broader range of responsibilities, including:

- Recruitment and nominations
- Orientation of new members
- Ongoing training and development for all trustees
- Board evaluation
- Planning the annual board retreat
- Paying attention to board dynamics and helping to resolve conflicts, if necessary
- Encouraging a culture of fun and mutual appreciation

In short, the board renewal committee helps to take care of the board, or more correctly stated, helps the board to better take care of itself.

This, one could argue, is the most important committee. It helps to recruit the best candidates, builds their skills, pays attention to their needs, and ensures an atmosphere of mutual support and respect. By doing its work effectively, it makes the entire board more productive.

12

Five Options for Board Orientation

Joining a board without being oriented is like landing in a foreign country without a map or any knowledge of local language and customs. You might find yourself at your first meeting, trying to decipher strange acronyms or wondering why everyone is giggling at in-jokes you don't understand.

Lacking proper orientation, new trustees are forced to sit on the sidelines for months or even years while they attempt to piece together their roles and responsibilities. It's a uniquely frustrating experience – being asked to lead without a basic understanding of how leadership works in a particular organization.

Rather than put new board members in this precarious and unnecessary position, your board renewal committee (or some other sub-group of the board) can design an orientation process that addresses the needs of incoming trustees. Here are five ways to give your new recruits a running start. Use these strategies individually or in combination: mix, match, and create your own approach.

1) *Board orientation book.* Many nonprofits present new board members with a three-ring binder filled with copies of the bylaws, articles of incorporation, board agreement, list of committees and their functions, minutes from recent meetings, an annual report, financial statements, recent newsletters and brochures, and the like. In a single resource, a new board member can easily find all the documents needed to understand, manage, and promote the organization.

2) *Orientation event.* Gather new leaders together – for no more than two hours – to talk them through the book, answer questions, introduce them to staff, give a tour of the facility if you have one, and meet with clients/customers/audience members who can offer their perspective on the value of your organization's work.

3) *The buddy system.* Ask each continuing board member to mentor one incoming trustee. This task would include a personal visit, phone calls after the first few meetings to debrief what happened, and being available to answer questions one-on-one as needed.

Given the inevitable changes in your organization's circumstances and programs, even seasoned board members need to be reoriented from time to time. Consider adding the following two options to your orientation menu.

4) *Annual "day in the office."* Encourage all trustees, both new and continuing, to volunteer one day per year to shadow a staff member whose work they know little about. By participating in the daily flow of work, trustees will gain a much better understanding of how the agency operates. Ideally, staff should pick a relatively interesting and varied day.

5) *Board retreat.* Many groups schedule an annual retreat – away from the usual meeting place – to discuss strategic issues that don't get addressed at regular board meetings. A retreat could focus on long-range planning, or changing your mix of programs, or marketing, or expanding your capacity to earn income by charging for your services.

Depending on the topic, it may be wise to schedule the retreat when new trustees are available. By starting them off with serious, substantive discussions – and not just the usual board business – incoming leaders will begin their service with a deeper understanding of your mission and your work.

13

Encouraging Turnover

The value of term limits

If you think back to Chapter 2, you'll remember how board roles and responsibilities evolve as nonprofits grow and change. The founding leaders may not necessarily be the right team to manage a growing staff, oversee expanding programs, or respond to significant changes in the marketplace. Even in well-established organizations, assumptions about community needs and how to best meet them must be regularly reviewed and challenged.

With this in mind, it continues to surprise and sadden me when I hear about board members who serve 10, 20, or even 30 years with the same organization. What can they possibly be thinking? Here's my best guess:

- "I'm irreplaceable. No one else can do what I do."

- "I embody organizational history. If I leave, nobody will remember the past, and we will be doomed to repeat it."

• "I'm a martyr. No one else will carry this burden."

• "It's a big part of my social life, and I enjoy regular opportunities to see my friends."

• "I'm going to stick around until the organization achieves X. Then I can leave knowing things will be fine without me." (Note: X is often a moving target.)

These internal monologues ignore the ways in which we all get stuck in our own particular ruts: the same actions (or inaction), the same assumptions and biases, the same interpersonal behaviors.

Nonprofit organizations are growing, changing organisms, and they need leaders with the capacity to envision the future in different ways. If your board doesn't change on a regular basis, organizational vision remains the same – and that can be deadly.

The concept of term limits has become popular with nonprofits. Under the typical model, trustees are limited to a specific number of consecutive years on the board. The most common configurations are three 2-year terms, or two 3-year terms, for a total of six years in a row. At that point, board members "term out" or cycle off the board.

If they wish to remain active, departing trustees can continue to serve on committees, assuming you include non-board committee members. Or they can take on specific tasks as assigned by the trustees: lead the capital campaign, organize a speaker's bureau, conduct focus groups with clients. Or, when called upon, they can serve as informal advisors to the board.

A "termed out" trustee can even rejoin the board after taking a year off, though this behavior defeats the purpose of limiting board service.

Term limits cannot be mandated by a book or an outside expert – they need to be discussed and debated. On this issue, as with many others, reasonable people can credibly disagree. If you decide to institute term limits, you'll need to amend the bylaws, which may require a vote of your membership.

14

How to Create a Great Agenda

(And then cancel the meeting)

Many trustees confuse going to meetings with fulfilling their duties. Alas, attending meetings barely qualifies as work – especially when you consider the typical agenda.

A report, a few questions, another report, another question or two, a digression, a discussion about which color to paint the office, and an argument about the wording of the spring appeal letter. All accompanied by stale coffee and crumbly cookies. A few hours of this drudgery and even the most vibrant board members will lapse into a coma.

You may not believe it, but important things *can* occur at board meetings: dreaming, planning, creating the future, figuring out how to pay for it. Perhaps a serious discussion breaks out and participants debate competing visions for the organization. Solving an immediate crisis can be a productive use of collective time, provided that it falls within the board's purview. (Neither paint color nor fundraising copy would qualify, and neither constitutes an emergency.)

Many board members like to complain about fruitless meetings. Because I am one of them, let me state my bias as clearly as I can: *the primary purpose of meetings is to make decisions.* Yes, you can use them to share information, but there are so many other ways to do that: by phone, through the mail, via email, on your website.

Sure, meetings help to build community and cohesion within the board, but only if they are substantive, satisfying, and productive. Pulling people together for the sake of form – "According to the bylaws, we must meet every month" – is a victory of form over substance. Victories like that will suffocate your organization.

How can you design a lively meeting that focuses on decision-making? It all begins with the agenda. Use the following template to create your own column heads, then fill in the appropriate information:

Time	Topic	Who?	Decision to be made	Follow-up needed	Who?	Deadline
When item begins		Discussion leader			(Will follow up)	

Here's an example for one agenda item; a complete sample agenda appears in the Appendix.

Time	Topic	Who?	Decision to be made	Follow-up needed	Who?	Deadline
8:15	Affordable housing ordinance - City Council meeting, 10/30	Bettina	Do we sign on as co-sponsor? If so, what resources can we commit?	Phone coalition partners to inform them of decision; assign rep to working group	Bettina and ??	Phone calls this week; working group meets 10/11

The most important column is the one in the middle: *Decision to be made.* In preparing the agenda, think carefully about this. What choices do we need to make? Do we need to make them now? If so, why?

Try building your agenda using this model. If nothing fits into the decision column – "Approve minutes of last meeting" does not qualify as a decision – consider two alternatives:

1) Add a meaty topic that requires a meaningful decision (and reduce or remove other items accordingly).

2) Cancel the meeting and use other avenues to share information among the trustees.

This agenda design also helps trustees understand that their responsibilities don't end when the meeting is over. Ideally, everyone leaves the room with an assignment or two to be completed before the next get-together. A portion of the subsequent meeting can be used to report on everyone's work, and then the group moves on to the next set of decisions.

At the very least, this template can be used to frame a discussion about how to make your meetings more effective. It's an important conversation, regardless of whether you choose to adopt, adapt, or disregard this model.

15

Building Consensus

In my work with nonprofits, I'm always mystified by the pervasive use and abuse of parliamentary procedure, also known as Robert's Rules of Order. Many, many board members believe that their discussions and decisions are somehow more valid when they make motions, second those motions, call the question, and hold formal votes that are recorded in the minutes.

Furthermore, people who know the Rules – or think they know the Rules – often use their alleged know-how as a way to exercise power within the group. "That's out of order," bellows the board bully. "You need to raise a point of order if you're going to reopen discussion on that motion, and you can't do that because we've already accepted an amendment to the original motion."

In response, everyone else feels sheepish, looks confused, and refuses to speak. All sorts of petty arguments arise from the ignorance or abuse of parliamentary procedure.

There is no law mandating that nonprofits must make decisions using Robert's Rules. After all, you're not a parliament. You're an animal shelter, or a sports league, or a theater, or an advocacy organization.

By way of comparison, imagine you're sitting around with a group of friends, trying to decide on a place for dinner. You discuss the options; people advocate for one restaurant or another. Perhaps you reach a tentative decision. At that point, someone opts out, saying, "I had Thai for lunch, but if that's what everybody wants, please go and enjoy yourselves." Maybe the rest of you decide to go, but more likely you return to the list to try to identify another option that will work for everyone.

The decision-making model you're using is called *consensus,* and it works something like this:

1) Someone presents an idea. It could be a formal proposal, but most of the time it's just an idea, not yet fully formed.

2) The idea is passed around and the pros and cons are discussed.

3) As a result of the discussion – the more input, the better – the idea is often modified.

4) If a general agreement seems to be emerging (this is where good listening and facilitation skills are helpful), you can test for consensus by restating the

latest version of the idea or proposal to see if everybody agrees.

5) If anyone dissents, you return to the discussion to see if you can modify the idea further to make it acceptable to everyone.

Unlike parliamentary procedure, which results in an up-or-down, yes-or-no vote, the consensus process allows for (and even encourages) a continuum of responses. At one end is strong endorsement: "Great idea. I love it!" At the other end is strong disagreement: "It's a horrible idea, and I'll do everything I can to block it."

The consensus spectrum allows for more subtle reactions: "I like it pretty well" to "I don't like it, but I can live with it" to "I disagree, but if you're all in favor, I won't stand in the way." This is an intuitive way to make decisions, since it reflects how most of us make shared choices in our daily lives.

In the traditional consensus model, one person has the power to block the decision if they strongly disagree. If the board is unable to create a compromise to satisfy the blocker, they may call for a majority vote as a last resort. This is sometimes known as "modified consensus," and for groups that want to try out consensus, it may be the best way to begin.

Be aware that consensus decision-making is often time-consuming and requires patience and persistence. On the other hand, it creates a more informal and equitable environment where everyone's voice is valued. From my perspective, this is an excellent trade-off.

For more tips and tools on this topic, see the excellent *Facilitator's Guide to Participatory Decision-Making* by Community at Work, www.communityatwork.com.

16

Deliberation vs. Action

I once served on the board of a nonprofit with only one program staff and no administrator. Nearly all administrative tasks – emptying the mailbox, correspondence, depositing checks, preparing the financial statements, arranging for insurance, updating the database, creating board materials, sending thank you notes, writing and printing and mailing the newsletter – fell to the trustees and other volunteers.

Our board members offered many admirable ideas about how to move the organization forward and manage it more effectively. The problem was, we had more ideas than time and energy to implement them, and insufficient funds to hire an administrator to relieve us of some of our monthly chores. We spent hours debating actions that we ultimately didn't have the capacity to carry out. As you can imagine, our meetings sometimes ended in frustration.

Were I still a trustee on that board, I would propose

the following policy: All suggestions made at board meetings must be followed by the phrase, "If my idea is approved, this is what I am PERSONALLY willing to do to implement it." A suitable variation would be, "I am willing to RECRUIT someone to do it, and will find that person by [date]."

Perhaps this is an unfair standard. After all, one of your duties as a trustee is to deliberate: to weigh and measure a wide range of options, including those that may seem impractical or overly ambitious. On the other hand, if your board spends a lot of time debating ideas that are not "actionable" because you don't have the resources to take action – well, you may not be using your time wisely.

"We don't have the resources" often means "we don't have the money," which is a solvable problem. For actionable ideas on boards and fundraising, see Chapters 18 to 22.

17

Committees

Don't overdo It

Why do nonprofit organizations have committees? Take the following quiz:

A) Because certain kinds of work are best done in smaller groups, trustees rely on committees to think through the opportunities and provide guidance to the board.

B) The committee structure is a way to involve outsiders and expand the pool of committed volunteers.

C) Organizations use committees as a way to develop new leaders who can be moved up to the board of directors some day.

D) A committee structure is mandated in the bylaws.

If you answered A, B, or C, you're correct. If you answered D, you're missing the point.

Many nonprofits abuse the intent of committees

by making them permanent; we sometimes call these *standing committees*. They're required to meet regularly, regardless of whether they have important work to do at that particular moment. An alternative model is to recruit small groups as needed – *work groups* or *task forces* – to accomplish specific tasks, report to the board, and disband.

Here are a few examples of how to use temporary work groups. They can:

• Organize and evaluate your annual fundraising event.

• Review your bylaws and suggest changes to the trustees.

• Study an emerging program issue and provide analysis to the full board.

• Create a job description for your first executive director and guide the hiring process.

Small, informal organizations tend to operate this way without even thinking about it. They identify problems that need to be addressed, then recruit problem-solvers: "Who wants to work on this?" If they're smart, they identify work-group leaders on the spot and schedule the first meeting.

After that, the work group is on its own to complete the task and bring their results back to the board for discussion, modification, and approval. In many instances, larger organizations would also benefit from the use of informal work groups, rather than creating formal committees to address every need.

Having sung the praises of informality, I must acknowledge that some committee work is ongoing and calls for the creation and maintenance of standing committees. Here's my suggested short list:

Executive. Usually comprised of the board officers, the executive committee is responsible for any decisions that must be made between board meetings, including preparation of meeting agendas. The purpose of this committee is *not* to reduce the power of the board as a whole, but rather to guide the board and make interim decisions as needed

Board governance or *board development* or *board renewal.* As discussed in Chapter 11, this committee is responsible for board recruitment and nominations, orientation of new members, ongoing training and development for all trustees, board evaluation, planning the annual board retreat, paying attention to board dynamics, and helping to resolve conflicts.

Development or *fundraising.* This committee leads fundraising planning, works with the full board to develop a list of participation options, and helps trustees follow through on their fundraising commitments.

Other committees may be appropriate for your

nonprofit. For example, some groups have a standing *program committee* to monitor programs – although I would argue that, in many cases, this is the work of the full board.

Other organizations create a *finance committee* to oversee the accounts (undoubtedly a good idea if you're handling a lot of money), or a *marketing committee* to generate more publicity, or a *personnel committee* to ensure that employees are treated fairly.

Still other groups raising money for buildings or an endowment may be guided by a *capital campaign* or an *endowment campaign committee.*

In closing, let me repeat that there's no official list of required committees, so design your own mix. Which ones make the most sense for your organization? Secondly, don't create standing committees if you don't have substantive work for them to do throughout the year. Design a less formal structure to complete the tasks that need to be done.

18

Give Generously

People are paying attention

When it comes to your fundraising responsibilities, the first priority is to give as generously as you can. As a leader, your time is the most valuable thing you can offer, but your financial support is also a high priority.

Let me be clear: I don't believe in a quota system or a "price" for joining the board, because you need a board that's diverse in all ways, including social class. But I am suggesting – nay, insisting – that all trustees contribute financially, even if the most they can donate is $25 or $50.

I could name a dozen reasons why this is essential, but let me focus on three:

1) It's a lot easier to raise money if you give it yourself. Indeed, if you're willing to discuss your own contribution with prospective donors – "Jan and I gave $500 this year, which is a big gift for us" – you will achieve instant credibility.

2) Frankly, it's an important way to test the commitment of board members. If you aren't willing to invest some of your own money, how committed are you?

3) Sooner or later, a foundation official, corporate giving officer, or individual major donor will inquire about board giving. If you can't brag about "100 percent board participation," the prospect will look at you and say, "Hey, if you can't get your own folks to give, why should I give?" In other words, if trustees choose to withhold their support, however modest it may be, their resistance could end up costing your group thousands of dollars in outside funding.

Someone must insist that all trustees make a personal gift. This can be done by the board chair, or the head of the fundraising committee, or a widely respected trustee with no particular title. The most passionate "asker" is always your best option, regardless of position or office.

Some nonprofits make this request at a board meeting, while others send personal letters. Still others schedule appointments to meet with each board member face to face or by phone. Some groups combine these approaches: for example, announcing at a board meeting that it's time for trustees to make their annual gift, then following up with each person on the telephone.

When setting the bar for board members, try using

this language in your board agreement. Then repeat it verbally when you ask:

"Because you're a leader in this organization, we expect to be one of the top three charities you support this year."

Seems fair, doesn't it? This approach encourages a range of contributions based on a range of income and financial ability. It's also built on the honor system – you're not going to sneak a look at anybody's check book or bank records to compare their donations to other nonprofits.

Without setting quotas or excluding anyone, this statement defines a clear, unambiguous expectation and encourages "stretch gifts" from everyone.

19

Why Board Members Can't (or Won't) Raise Money

"How many of you are satisfied with your board's fundraising results?"

When I ask this question at workshops, it generates lots of ironic laughter. In my experience, the great majority of boards do a poor job raising money. Indeed, if most trustees embraced their fundraising responsibilities with commitment and good humor, consultants like me would have a lot less work.

Since fundraising is an essential (and often inescapable) responsibility, you must deal with any reluctance head-on. The simplest and most direct way is to pose the question I use in my trainings: "What barriers get in the way of your full, active participation?" Here are some typical responses:

1) *"I don't know anyone who has money."* This common belief is factually incorrect. Seventy percent of Americans donate to charity, including many middle-class, working-class, and poor people. The median amount they contribute is between $1,300 and $2,000 per year. We all know donors – lots of them – and these folks are more generous than we imagine.

If you believe that much of this money goes to faith organizations (churches, mosques, synagogues), you're correct. These groups collect about one-third of all charitable dollars.

Why? They ask often, they build strong relationships with their constituents, and they don't discriminate between the rich and the poor – they ask everyone. If churches stopped requesting donations from middle-income and poor people, and relied solely on the rich, many would go out of business.

When it comes to fundraising, don't think of faith organizations as competition – study them as role models.

2) *"I don't want to ask my friends and bring money into the relationship."* In my informal polling, I've discovered that many of us are already asking people we know for charitable contributions, and nothing bad is happening to our relationships. Because our friends tend to share our values, our work as volunteers is a source of pride and inspiration to them.

They want to help.

The solution is simple enough. When you approach friends, let them know that it's fine to say no. Be explicit about it. State that you will respect their decision, whatever it is, and that your relationship will not change if they choose not to participate.

For example, you might say, "Sally, I'm on the board of this terrific organization. One of my tasks is to raise money. I was hoping you could help with a donation of $___. If you have other priorities, I certainly respect that. We will remain friends regardless of what you decide. But I sure hope you can help."

3. *"Fundraising is not my job."* When recruiting board members, be clear that yes, fundraising is one aspect of board work and everyone is expected to help. Because fundraising is a team sport, the more people you involve, the more money you raise. Conversely, when board members fail to embrace this responsibility, your capacity to generate income is severely reduced.

4. *"Nobody asked me to raise money."* See the previous item.

5. *"I don't know how."* Fair enough; no one comes out of the womb raising money. You must emphasize that trustees will be supported in their efforts, and then back up that promise with training, tools, and appreciation.

• • •

Undoubtedly you could come up with a longer list

of barriers, resistance points, and excuses. However real these barriers may (or may not) be, they don't hide the essential fact: your group needs money, and it's your job to help raise it.

Happily, there are many ways to productively participate. The next chapter will help you choose the options that will work best for you and your colleagues.

20

One Solution: The Board Fundraising Menu

Novices equate the word "fundraising" with "the ask" – the moment when the gift is requested in person, at an event, through the mail, or by phone.

But taken holistically, fundraising (some professionals prefer the words *development* or *stewardship*) is really a cycle of activities that includes identifying prospective donors, educating and cultivating them, asking for their support, recognizing their contribution, and deepening their commitment by engaging them in the organization's mission.

Given this framework, a lot of activities can be included in the behavior we call "fundraising."

Try this exercise. Ask your board to brainstorm all the ways they could assist with any sort of fundraising. Encourage them to think creatively, because the goal is to come up with the longest list possible. Here are several likely items:

- Give money themselves
- Include your organization in their wills
- Identify prospects: friends, family, acquaintances, co-workers, and so on
- Sign fundraising letters and add personal notes
- "Open doors" by setting up appointments to meet with prospective donors
- Participate in donor meetings (even if the trustee wants someone else to make the ask)
- Host a fundraising house party
- Organize fundraising events or donor recognition events
- Sell event or raffle tickets
- Write thank you notes
- Serve as an ambassador by talking about your nonprofit in the community
- Organize a board fundraising training
- Serve on the development committee to help create a fundraising plan
- Assist with grantseeking by researching grant opportunities, writing proposals, and meeting with funders
- Figure out ways to earn income by charging for your services

To help you think beyond the obvious, here's one

creative way board members can support the fundraising process while avoiding the dreaded "ask."

Imagine the following phone call: "Harvey, my name is Andy Robinson. I'm a volunteer board member with [name of group]. I'm not calling tonight to ask for money" – take a pause while the donor sighs with relief – "I'm just calling to say thank you. You made a generous contribution a few months ago and I believe you received a thank you letter from the office. I just wanted to add my personal thanks. Do you have any questions about our work? Would you like to be involved in any way? OK, that's all for now. I just wanted to check in and say thanks. We really appreciate your support. Have a good evening."

If you end up talking to the voice mail, no problem; simply leave the same message.

Imagine that five of your board members agree to make three or four of these calls per month, investing a total of fifteen minutes per month. By the end of the year, you will make *personal contact with 200 to 300 donors.*

Now imagine what will happen when you later approach those supporters for a renewal gift. You're right: they'll be very responsive.

With your brainstormed list in hand, work together as a board to prioritize the top 8 to 10 items. Even if you're not seasoned fundraisers, you're likely to identify at least some of the best strategies, because most are self-evident: give money, provide names of prospects, add personal notes to letters, ask people you know, and so on.

As the author and trainer Joan Flanagan once said, "All the knowledge about fundraising can be summed up in a few words: Ask 'em, thank 'em, ask 'em again, thank 'em again. And give money yourself."

As you'll learn in the next chapter, you can use this list to help each trustee prepare a personalized fundraising agreement that meets his or her specific needs, interests, and limitations.

21

Board Fundraising Agreements

Another barrier to successful board fundraising is the tendency to require all trustees to participate in the same activities and meet the same benchmarks: identify 20 prospects, sell 20 raffle tickets, apologize 20 times when asking for money, and so forth. Since we all begin with varied interests, abilities, and levels of commitment, a regimented approach like this is bound to fail.

To remove the barrier, help your board members create *personalized fundraising agreements* that meet their needs, honor their limitations, and encourage them to participate in a meaningful way.

Here's how it works. After putting your heads together to develop the menu and prioritize options as discussed in the last chapter, board members take turns choosing:

- Their preferred strategies
- Timing – when they would like to be involved
- How much money they believe each activity will raise
- Any help they might need from other trustees and staff to complete their commitment

To make this work, you'll need to identify and prepare a few board members to speak first, show some enthusiasm, and be specific. These leaders set the proper tone, which helps other trustees to get over any resistance or self-consciousness about verbalizing their commitments. Your goal is to develop an agreement that looks something like this:

> I, Andy Robinson, agree to:
>
> - Donate $50 per month for the next year, for a total annual gift of $600. I will provide my bank account information so the gift can be deducted automatically each month from my account. I will need the staff to help with the paperwork.
>
> - In November, I will mail holiday letters asking my friends and family to make contributions to our organization instead of sending me more holiday gifts I don't need. I will write the letter, but would like someone else to look it over before I send it. I expect that 10 people will respond with donations of $25 each, for a total of $250.
>
> - Join staff on five major donor visits between January and March. I don't know how much money these meetings will yield, but I hope that one donor

will give $500 and another $1,000. I'll do my best to help identify prospects, but I am willing to meet with individuals I don't know, as long as staff sets up the meetings.

The conversation continues around the table with each person laying out his or her individual fundraising plan. While this is happening, someone types notes into the computer. After everyone has spoken, print these documents and have them signed by the chair and each respective board member. Then make photocopies for the individual trustees, the staff, and the board leader – perhaps the chair of the fundraising committee – who will oversee follow-through on these commitments.

The board fundraising agreement reinforces the idea that everyone must participate, but allows a range of choices in *how* they participate. It shifts the discussion from, "Will you help with fundraising?" to "*How* will you help with fundraising?"

For a more detailed description of this strategy, see the article "53 Ways for Board Members to Raise $1,000" by Kim Klein, available from the *Grassroots Fundraising Journal*, www.grassrootsfundraising.org.

22

Setting Goals for Board Giving and Getting

With any volunteer activity, including board service, there is often a gap between intention and results. Board members tend to make commitments they can't keep. Most people want to do the right thing, but it's also easy to avoid tasks they don't really want to do, such as raising money.

To encourage accountability and follow-through, consider setting collective goals for:

• *Board giving* – how much trustees donate from their own pockets – and

• *Board fundraising* – how much you collectively raise from other sources.

These goals can be included as specific line items in your annual operating budget.

The first goal requires a frank discussion at the beginning of the budget year. "If we combine our personal gifts," the trustees are asked, "how much do we think we can give? Are we a $2,000 board? A $10,000 board? What number should we shoot for?" If desired, each individual's gift can remain confidential because it is blended into the shared number.

The best strategy is to debate the number, set a tentative goal, hand out pledge forms, ask each trustee to write down the amount of his or her annual gift, and collect the forms.

The board chair, perhaps joined by fundraising staff, leaves the room, tallies up the gifts, and returns to the meeting to report the total. If the goal is met, everybody cheers. If not, trustees can choose to dig a little deeper, which is usually the best choice, or lower the target to reflect the current reality.

The second line item – board fundraising – can be handled in a similar way: add up each individual's fundraising commitments (see the previous chapter) to reach a collective target for how much money board members will raise on their own initiative.

For example, trustees can decide to seek donations to underwrite a specific line item in the budget – maybe you want to fund a new part-time staff position, or there's a piece of equipment you really need in the clinic – and then create a fundraising campaign around that line item or project.

By designating budget lines for board giving and board fundraising, you increase accountability. Each time trustees review the budget, these line items stand out. If the board benchmarks aren't being met, it's nearly impossible to blame the staff.

23

How to fix it

Poor Attendance at Meetings

Beyond the usual complications of family, work, and other commitments – in other words, not enough time – the primary reason people fail to show up at meetings is that the meetings aren't productive. Nothing of consequence happens. As a result, absentees don't feel they're missing anything important.

The best solution is to create interesting, challenging agendas that focus on decision-making. For tips on how to do this effectively, see chapter 14. A sample agenda is also included on page 110.

Other ideas to improve your turnout include the following:

Hold fewer meetings. If you gather monthly, try ten meetings per year. Make each one count a little more.

Schedule many months in advance. If you meet on a regular date – for example, the second Monday of the month – ask trustees to confirm the dates and put them in their calendars at least six months in advance.

Distribute the agenda beforehand. At least one week before the meeting, email or mail the agenda with a reminder about the date, time, and location. Hint: controversial agenda items always boost turnout.

Use your board agreement to reinforce attendance requirements. Include language such as, "Three consecutive unexcused absences will be considered resignation from the board."

Feed people. It's one of the oldest ways to express appreciation. If cost is a concern, rotate this task among the board members and ask them to take turns covering the expense.

Include a "mission moment." Author and consultant Kay Sprinkel Grace advises that every time you gather, include a personal testimonial from a client, or a video excerpt from your recent performance, or a brief slide show about the land your organization just preserved – something tangible to re-connect trustees with the mission and remind them why they serve.

Rotate responsibility for chairing or facilitating the meeting. If necessary, provide training and support.

When participants know their turn is coming, they'll show up to watch how others manage the process and learn from their peers.

Yes, groups probably hold too many meetings. And yes, we could probably dispense with half of them. In the end, it's not about the quantity, but rather the quality. If you make them lively, substantive, and challenging, and you create opportunities for everyone to participate in a meaningful way, people will show up.

24

How to fix it

Poor Follow-through on Commitments

I hear a lot of complaints about boards, but perhaps the most common one centers around promises not kept. "I'll take care of it," says the well-meaning trustee – and then life gets in the way. The task slides further and further down the to-do list. Eventually it falls off the list altogether.

As a well-intentioned board member prone to over-commitment, I have empathy for people on both sides of this problem. As I write this, I'm thinking about the board work I've been avoiding this week. (No surprise – it has to do with fundraising.) But as someone who frequently relies on the work of others, I can also feel frustrated and angry when they don't honor their agreements.

First and foremost, we must respect the fact that

we trustees serve as *volunteers* and calibrate our expectations accordingly. We can't require people to devote the same amount of time or energy or love as they give to their families, their livelihoods, their health and well-being.

Here are a few thoughts to keep you and your fellow volunteers firmly on task:

Negotiate clear guidelines for how much time you expect from each other. This begins with recruitment, but should be revisited at least once a year with the full board. For more details on this topic, see Chapter 7.

Develop and use a board job description. Make sure you have a written agreement that outlines mutual expectations. When you sit down to talk about time, take a look at this document to ensure that it remains accurate and relevant. Job descriptions are covered in detail in Chapters 5 and 6, and a sample appears in the Appendix.

Clarify and test all assumptions by saying them out loud. Often, one person may hear the word "commitment" while the other is really saying, "I'll try to complete this task, but it's a low priority right now." Paraphrase what you've heard to make sure you understand it correctly.

Build "time off" into the board calendar. This can be done collectively: "Since we tend to get less work done in August, let's agree not to make any commitments that month." As an alternative, free time could be allocated on a rotating basis: "Anna's daughter is visiting for two weeks in April, so she's requested no extra board work that month. Who's got a busy stretch coming and wants to claim May as time off?"

Be sure everyone leaves each meeting with a specific task to complete before the next meeting – and then ask them to report on their work when you reconvene. Trustees who avoid or resist this approach will eventually leave your board, making room for new talent, passion, and dedication.

25

How to fix it

Micro-Management and Confusion about Roles

Inexperienced boards tend to work at the wrong "altitude" by focusing on details better left to staff. This problem is often compounded in small, understaffed organizations; one minute the board is engaged in long-term planning, while the next they're leading hikes, painting the office, volunteering on the telephone hot line, and dragging chairs around for the annual meeting. This creates confusion about the function of the board and who is supervising whom.

As I hope I've made clear in this book, the principal role of the board is oversight and planning. The staff (if you have staff) implements the plan through daily operations.

If you find that these lines are blurry, here are several suggestions to address the problem:

Clarify the chain of command. In the traditional model, the board supervises the executive director or CEO, who in turn supervises other staff. You can modify this arrangement – for example, the development committee may have a role in updating your fundraising plan and making recommendations directly to program staff – but first discuss the pros and cons with fellow trustees and create a clear policy.

Clarify who is supervising whom, and accept that roles may change depending on the activity. In grassroots organizations, sometimes board members function as leaders: providing vision, evaluating results, overseeing the finances. At these moments, they serve as guides and supervisors to the lead staff.

At other times, they do the work of regular volunteers: sitting behind a table at community events, phoning donors for renewal gifts, or writing thank you notes. In these moments, they need to accept guidance from staff or whomever is organizing the activity, and not abuse their power as trustees by undercutting or second-guessing their colleagues.

If you find yourselves having conflicts about roles, choose a non-controversial issue to work through the question of micro-management. Pick a hypothetical issue – not the one causing the immediate controversy – and use it to frame a conversation about the board's role. Under those circumstances, what would be appropriate (or inappropriate) board behavior? If you can sort this out at an emotional distance and create guidelines that everyone accepts, it will be much easier to deal with the "live" conflict.

Seek outside help. If the problem persists, you may want a consultant or an experienced and respected trustee from another organization to help your board resolve it. An outsider can provide a neutral, dispassionate perspective about where to draw the line between trustee authority and staff responsibility.

26

How to fix it

Personal Agendas and Conflicts of Interest

Every now and then someone will join a nonprofit board to re-create the world in his or her own image. However, the vast majority of trustees assume their responsibilities with good intentions and a degree of humility.

If they weren't concerned about a community issue – maybe even one that affects them personally – they probably wouldn't have joined the board. Perhaps they want to reduce pollution in the neighborhood, or create an opportunity for their kids to play in an orchestra, or cure a disease that afflicts a family member.

To state this differently, self-interest isn't inherently a bad thing. It can be a powerful force for good. Still, there will be times when personal needs and desires are at odds with organizational goals, and this can lead to serious problems in governance.

If you begin with the assumption of goodwill and reasonable motives, it will be a lot easier to reach a consensus about conflicts of interest. Here's how to do it.

Try to define inappropriate behavior before it begins. It's unlikely that you can tackle this subject in the course of a regular meeting, so put it on the agenda for your next board retreat.

As outlined in the previous chapter on micro-management, pick a hypothetical conflict of interest that might come up in your work. If you're a trustee of a school, how far can you go to promote a school policy that would benefit a subset of the students, including your own child?

If you're working to conserve open space, how would you prioritize protection of adjacent land that could increase the monetary value of your own property? Create examples to debate, then use these examples to develop a policy that applies to all board members.

Request conflict of interest policies from sister organizations. How do other nonprofits deal with this question? What can you learn from them? You may need staff assistance to gather this information for board review.

Study relevant guidelines from professional associations and networks. If your group belongs to a peer network or is evaluated by a credentialing agency, ask for a template or a list of criteria that cover this issue. As above, this research needs to be undertaken jointly by staff and board.

Name it. If you believe a trustee has crossed the line by promoting his or her self-interest, take responsibility and raise the issue. As a first step, talk with the person individually, perhaps accompanied by the board chair. (You will get better results if you begin with an inquisitive, rather than confrontational, approach.)

If this strategy fails, you may need to bring your concerns to the attention of the full board. This is much easier to do if trustees have discussed the topic in advance and developed clear guidelines.

Recuse yourself. If you and your colleagues agree that you have a conflict of interest, step aside while others make the relevant decision. If necessary, the board can create a benchmark to trigger this recusal.

For example, if two-thirds of the trustees perceive a conflict of interest, the relevant board member(s) would be required to step aside for that vote or other decision-making process.

•••

Unfortunately, if you need a vote to sort these things out, you haven't done your homework. Most problems relating to personal agendas and conflicts of interest can and should be resolved much sooner – through clear expectations, open conversations, and a written policy to back it up. You also need to cover these issues when recruiting and orienting new trustees.

27

How to fix it

Inactive Board Members Who Really Need to Leave

As in professional sports and politics and any number of endeavors, some folks hang on way too long – long after their passion is gone, long after they have anything new to offer.

As outlined in Chapter 13, I'm a strong proponent of term limits for board members – in other words, mandatory retirement. Particularly valuable trustees can return to the board after a year or two off, but the practice of term limits institutionalizes turnover and forces the board to seek out new blood, new energy, and new ideas.

If you don't yet have such a policy, and your trustees just won't go away, consider the following options.

Develop and institute a board job description. Clarifying your mutual expectations and commitments – making them specific and tangible, rather than relying on assumptions – will help to level the playing field for all leaders.

Use this job description to initiate a self-evaluation process for all board members. Based on the evaluation, ineffective board members will sometimes re-commit to the work and improve their performance. In other cases, individuals who can't or won't meet the standards will take the opportunity to bow out. "It's a new era," they'll say, "and you're looking for things I can't provide." For more on board evaluation, see the next chapter.

Include specific criteria for meeting attendance – for example, "Three consecutive unexcused absences will be considered resignation from the board." If people stop showing up – and stop communicating about *why* they don't show up – you have explicit permission to replace them. Of course, it would be prudent to talk with them first about why they're missing so many meetings, and what this indicates about their desire and ability to serve on the board.

Create an "honorary board" or "emeritus board" for those leaving the governing board. If appropriate, you can keep the names of departing trustees on the letterhead and maintain their connection to the organization. They can even be assigned specific tasks – for example, organizing a donor recognition event or hosting a house party. But the honorary board has no role in governing or managing the organization.

Note: For this strategy to work, the honorary board must be perceived as a place of honor rather than a pile of deadwood. Begin by recruiting two or three well-respected former trustees who, by allowing you to use their names, will set the proper tone.

Live with it. You need a critical mass of effective board members – for grassroots groups, typically five or six active and committed people – to get the work done. If things are working reasonably well, you may decide to accept reality: not everyone will serve with the same level of passion and skill. Do the best you can with the folks you've got.

28

Evaluate Your Board, Evaluate Yourself

As a topic of interest – the kind that generates animated conversation – board evaluation is right up there with the technical specifications of sewer pumps. Sure, life would go on without sewer pumps, but it would be a lot less pleasant.

The same holds true with board evaluation – you can get by without talking about it, but wouldn't you rather know where you stand? A comprehensive evaluation can help you fix what's broken or reward yourselves for the things you do well. Indeed, many trustees come through an evaluation process with a degree of relief and pride. By taking a step back, they can see both the good and the bad more clearly, and gain a greater appreciation of both.

Any successful evaluation process should touch on the following topics:

• Progress toward organizational goals, including the development of benchmarks to measure that progress.

• Changes in the environment in which you operate – shifting demographics and community needs, funding, duplication of services, potential allies, and so forth – and how your nonprofit is adapting (or not) to these developments.

• A review of your decision-making process to ensure that it's open, equitable, and incorporates the voices of your constituents.

• A sense of how your trustees are faring in their roles: their successes, challenges, unmet needs, and personal growth on the job.

Many fine resources are available to help with your evaluation process. For starters, take a look at Gayle Gifford's *How Are We Doing?*, available from this publisher, and *Benchmarking Your Organization's Development*, from the Institute for Conservation Leadership, www.icl.org. Both books can help guide you through a thorough evaluation process.

29

If It's Not Fun, It's Not Worth It

At your board meetings, how much time is devoted to laughter?

I know, I know ... you're trying to end poverty, fight discrimination, clean up a polluted river, put a stop to domestic violence, cure horrible diseases, and expose government and corporate corruption. These are not funny subjects. Given the size and scope of these challenges, it's easy to get weighed down.

And yet...

The most effective boards make a point of having fun together – celebrating victories, honoring little accomplishments, laughing about the ironies of the work. Given the inordinate number of details and the slow pace of change, it's easy to burn out. Our work is made possible – and, I hope, enjoyable – through our common purpose, generosity of spirit, and our ability to smile in the face of adversity and inertia.

Make an effort to thank each other, even when the results aren't what you'd hoped for. Begin your next meeting with a potluck meal. If you're not faced with any immediate decisions, end the meeting early and go to the park together. Create silly annual awards for all the trustees – *Bravest Fundraiser, Least Likely to Respond to Email, Rookie of the Year, The Five Heads Award* (for most nonprofit hats). If you want to have a really good time, hand out kazoos and lead a rendition of the graduation theme, "Pomp and Circumstance," while the winners collect their certificates.

The point is this: all work and no play makes for a lousy board and an unproductive leadership experience. By having fun, you create a cohesive team where everyone feels valued and looks forward to spending time together.

The first board I ever served on – more than 20 years ago – had many of these qualities. Our goal was to harness the power of art to promote peace and nuclear disarmament. As you can imagine, this was a creative bunch – actors, writers, designers, visual artists – and it showed. But more than the concerts and rallies and performances, what I enjoyed most was our *esprit de corps*: the willingness to collectively pitch in and do what needed to be done.

For our annual board retreat, we spent the weekend

together on the coast. I'm sure we talked business and made plans for our next show, but what I remember most clearly are the long walks on the beach and a huge pot of spaghetti we all helped to prepare. Fresh tomatoes from somebody's garden, with lots and lots of garlic. Endless laughter around the kitchen table. Stories told and told again.

We came together on the board because we shared a vision for a better world, but our mutual affection – made tangible in a plate of pasta – was what sustained us.

What sustains *you*? Whatever it is, share it with your fellow trustees. As with any experience in life, you get out what you put in, so share the best parts of yourself: compassion, wisdom, humor, gratitude. And don't forget to bring the food.

APPENDIX

The Official Documents

(And how to use them)

If your group is a 501(c)(3) nonprofit – the charitable, tax-exempt variety most common in the U.S. – you should possess three essential documents:

1) Articles of incorporation are issued by your state government. This document recognizes your status as a nonprofit corporation, briefly states your charitable purpose, and lists your founding trustees.

2) Bylaws, which you prepared yourselves (or perhaps adapted from a model) and submitted to the state with your incorporation papers. Bylaws outline how you govern yourselves. They typically cover board terms, list the leadership offices, and describe how board members and officers are chosen.

Bylaws can itemize requirements for board composition: for example, "at least 51 percent people with disabilities" or "a minimum of two youth below the age of 21." They can also include a discussion of how decisions are reached: through consensus, parliamentary procedure (Robert's Rules), or some other means. If at any time you want to amend the bylaws, see the bylaws, because they also include procedures for amendment.

3) Your federal tax ID letter, sometimes called a *501(c)(3) letter,* confirms your status as tax-exempt organization that may receive tax-deductible contributions. This class of organization includes houses of worship, colleges and private schools, social service agencies, arts and cultural groups, health agencies, international relief organizations, conservation and historic preservation groups, animal welfare organizations, community development organizations, and most advocacy groups.

Other nonprofits that do more direct lobbying may be classified as 501(c)(4), which means that they're tax-exempt, but donations they receive are not tax-deductible.

Keep these papers in a safe place, because you'll need them from time to time. Confused about board elections? Check the bylaws. Applying for a foundation grant? More often than not, the funders want to see your Federal tax letter – and perhaps your articles of incorporation as well.

However, don't assume these documents confer any particular wisdom or grace. They offer no guidance on the day to day operations of your organization, and are of little use in clarifying the roles and expectations of the board.

SAMPLE BOARD JOB DESCRIPTION

What board members provide

What board members can expect in return

1) I will give my best effort to "hit the ground running" when beginning my service with the board.

1) The organization will provide me a full orientation, including background information on work accomplished to date.

2) I will learn about the organization's mission and programs, and be able to describe them accurately.

2) The organization will provide me with relevant materials and education.

3) I understand that the board meets ___ times per year, plus one annual full-day retreat. I will do my best to attend each meeting, with the understanding that three consecutive unexcused absences will be considered resignation from the board.

3) I expect board meetings to be well run and productive, with a focus on decision-making, rather than reporting. I understand that agendas will be distributed at least one week in advance. If I wish to add items to the agenda, I will contact the chair at least two weeks in advance.

4) I accept fiduciary responsibility for the organization and will oversee its financial health and integrity.

4) I expect timely, accurate, and complete financial statements to be distributed at least quarterly, one week in advance of the relevant board meeting. I also expect to be trained to interpret these financial statements.

5) I will provide oversight to ensure that our programs run effectively.

5) I expect monthly reports from the executive director, program updates, press clippings, etc.

6) I accept ethical responsibility and will help to hold fellow board members, the executive director (and, by extension, the full staff) to professional standards.

6) The organization will provide me with relevant training.

(Continued)

What board members provide	What board members can expect in return
7) I will serve as an ambassador to the community to educate others and promote our work.	7. I will need materials and may need training (public speaking, etc.) to do this job effectively.
8. I commit to increasing my skills as a board member.	8. The organization will provide me with appropriate training and support.
9. I will participate in fundraising to ensure that our organization has the resources it needs to meet its mission. I commit to making a personal donation; our organization will be one of the top three charities I support each year that I am on the board.	9. I will be able to choose from a range of fundraising activities, and I expect relevant training and support to help me fulfill my obligations. I will have the option of fulfilling my personal pledge in monthly or quarterly installments, if I so choose.
10. I will evaluate the performance of the executive director.	10. This evaluation will be based on goals developed jointly by the board and the E.D.

Board member signature_____ **Date**_____

Board chair signature _____ **Date**_____

SAMPLE BOARD RECRUITMENT MATRIX

In the left column, fill in the skills and qualities you desire from your board members (see Chapter 8). Across the top, write the initials of your current board members, or simply rank the board as a whole. Here's a simple scoring system: + (outstanding), ✓ (adequate), - (poor), ? (don't know).

Skills & Qualities Desired   Board Member Initials

SAMPLE BOARD APPLICATION AND NOMINATION FORM

Adapted from Dogwood Alliance, www.dogwoodalliance.org. Used with permission.

Nominee _____

Nominator _____

Relationship of Nominee to Dogwood Alliance _____

Occupation _____ **Employer** _____

Address _____

Phone _____ **Email** _____

Do you support Dogwood Alliance's mission to protect Southern forests by building broad-based, diverse support for ending unsustainable industrial forestry practices?

           __Yes   __No

Why do you feel passionately about Dogwood Alliance's mission to protect Southern forests?

What will you bring to the board (for example, skills, expertise, constituency representation)?

Years willing to serve on Board of Directors: (if you choose fewer than four, you will be eligible to extend your service should you decide to stay on the board longer than two or three years)

           __ 2   __3   __4

Committee interests: Currently, we have four committees: program, fundraising, risk/audit, and the executive committee which covers financial management, personnel, nominations and board development. Most of the board's work happens at the committee level.

        __Financial   __Personnel   __Risk/Audit

        __Nominations and Board Development

          __Program   __Fundraising

Would you be willing to serve on the executive committee during one or more years of your term by chairing a committee or being an officer (Chair, Vice Chair, Treasurer, Secretary)? Most people will serve in a leadership role for at least one year.

        __Yes   __No   Which role(s)?

Are you able to attend the board orientation on (date)? Participation is required of all new board members.

__Yes   __No

Would you be willing to consider Dogwood Alliance number one or two among the nonprofits you support, in terms of your time and your financial contribution?

__Yes   __No

On which other boards do you serve?

Are you willing to raise funds for Dogwood Alliance, through whatever avenue you feel most comfortable (such as meetings or phone calls with donors, organizing events, giving presentations)?

__Yes   __No

Will you participate in the Annual Seed Project by suggesting the names of at least 10 friends, family and colleagues? Dogwood Alliance will provide fundraising letters for you to personalize (by adding handwritten notes) and send.

__Yes   __No

Are you willing to attend quarterly committee meetings by phone? Will you attend one full board conference call in July and two in-person, weekend meetings in March and November, usually held in Asheville? Conference calls last about one hour and are generally held in the evening. (Occasionally missing meetings is acceptable as long as you have notified the Chair or Committee Chair.)

__Yes   __No

Will you take the fiduciary responsibility of board members seriously and seek out guidance if you don't know how to read the financial statements?

__Yes   __No

Will you respect the Board's consensus decision-making process?

__Yes   __No

If the board does not elect you this year, are you willing to serve on a committee as a non-board member? If yes, which one:

__Fundraising   __Program   __Risk/Audit

SAMPLE MEETING AGENDA

Time	Topic	Who?	Decision to be made	Follow-up needed	Who?	Deadline
7:00	Welcome	Nancy				
7:05	Misson moment: slide show on Main St. project	Carlos				
7:20	Updates on individual fundraising since last meeting	All				
7:30	Presentation of draft fund-raising plan	Rod and Wanda	Approve or revise goals – do we have the right mix of strategies?	Update goals and plan based on board input	Rod, Wanda, and ???	November board meeting for final approval
8:15	Affordable housing ordinance – City Council meeting 10/30	Bettina	Do we sign on as a co-sponsor? If so, what resources can we commit?	Phone coalition partners to inform them of our decision; assign rep. to working group	Bettina and ???	Phone calls this week; working group meets 10/11
8:40	New business	Nancy				
8:55	Assign chair for next mtng; confirm other assignments	Nancy				Agenda to be distributed by 10/27
9:00	Thanks and adjourn	Nancy				

Also by Emerson & Church, Publishers

Raising Thousands (if Not Tens of Thousands) of Dollars with Email
by Madeline Stanionis • Emerson & Church, Publishers • $24.95

After reading the title of this book perhaps you're saying, "Sure, Red Cross and UNICEF can raise tons of money with email, but my agency isn't a brand name. You're telling me I can do the same!?" Author Madeline Stanionis isn't Pollyanna, but what she does convincingly show is that you can have surprising success if you approach email fundraising with intelligence and creativity.

Raising More Money with Newsletters than You Ever Thought Possible by Tom Ahern • Emerson & Church, Publishers • $24.95

Today, countless organizations are raising more money with their newsletter than with traditional mail appeals. And after reading this book, it's easy to understand why. For starters, the newsletters Ahern shows you how to write deliver real news, not tired features. They make the donor feel important. They use emotional triggers to spur action. They're designed in a way to attract both browsers and readers. And they don't depend on dry statistics.

Raising $1,000 Gifts by Mail by Mal Warwick • Emerson & Church, Publishers • $24.95

Whoever heard of raising $1,000 gifts (not to mention $5,000 gifts!) by mail? That's the province of personal solicitation, right? Not exclusively, says Mal Warwick. With carefully selected examples and illustrations, Warwick shows you how to succeed with high-dollar mail, walking you step by step through the process of identifying your prospects, crafting the right letter, the right brochure, the right response device, and the right envelope.

Raising Money through Bequests by David Valinsky & Melanie Boyd
Emerson & Church, Publishers • $24.95

Never in history has there been more money on the table for your organization than right now. As members of the "Greatest Generation" pass on, they're collectively leaving billions of dollars to charitable organizations. Their preferred vehicle for giving this money is the simple bequest – "I give and bequeath to...." With step by step guidance, and ample illustrations, this book shows you how to position your organization to be the beneficiary.

Emerson & Church, Publishers
www.emersonandchurch.com

Copies of this and other books from the publisher
are available at discount when purchased
in quantity for boards of directors or staff.

Emerson
& Church
PUBLISHERS

P.O. Box 338 • Medfield, MA 02052
508-359-0019 • www.emersonandchurch.com